BAD MEDICINE:
TALES OF MISCHIEF, MALICE, MURDER, AND MYSTERY

BY ALEC OLIVA

TABLE OF CONTENTS

Dedicated to Cathy L. Oliva

INTRODUCTION

Murder, greed, and dishonesty...all the sins we commonly associate with the lowest among us. Meanwhile, we associate lifesaving, altruism, and integrity with all those in our medical field. Our societal alter-casting, while benign and justifiable in many cases, can make us blind to the human nature of those we trust with our lives. At the end of the day, healthcare professionals are no less human than the patients they treat and, as such, they can fall victim to the darkest elements that are so deeply engrained in mankind. Occasionally, this can give rise to absolute and pure evil. Within this book are a few examples of some of the most infamous, sinful, and truly deplorable healthcare workers who ever lived.

It should be noted for the sake of caution, however, that these tales aren't meant to dissuade anyone from consulting medical professionals on a regular basis. Just as it is wrong to blindly accept that all healthcare workers are meticulous angels from above, these anecdotes should not be used to represent the many incredible men and women who work tirelessly to save lives each and every day.

CHAPTER 1:
THE BLACK DAHLIA

A SHOCKING DISCOVERY

O n the morning of January 15, 1947, a young mother, Betty Bersinger, walked her three-year-old daughter through their developing neighborhood in Los Angeles, California. At about 10:00 a.m., the two approached a vacant lot located at what is now 3825 Norton Avenue. From the woman's peripheral vision, she noticed a young, naked woman lying on the undeveloped, grassy property lot. Betty likely believed the woman had spent the previous evening drinking and, in a drunken stupor, concluded the night with a nap on the grass. However, as the mother and daughter neared the woman, Betty realized the truth was far more gruesome than she could ever have imagined. Lying on the grass, a young, pale woman with thick, dark brown hair, had been brutally murdered and mutilated. The body was separated in two; the torso had been surgically separated from the legs, staged in such a way to define the gory separation. Unusually, the body was spotless, as though the victim had been bathed after being murdered. Lacerations were located throughout the corpse. Perhaps the most spine-chilling of all, however, were the cuts made to the sides of the victim's mouth. The murderer, in an apparent attempt at dark humor, had left the victim with a permanent, bloody grin; deep lacerations spanning the corners of the victim's mouth to the base of her ears. The victim's intestines were neatly tucked beneath her buttocks, several deep cuts had been made on her breasts and thighs, and the victim's legs were spread apart with her hands and arms raised over her head, bent ninety degrees at the elbows. Ms. Bersinger desperately ran to the nearest home she could find and knocked furiously against their door. As soon as the homeowner opened their door, Betty rushed to the home's telephone and hysterically called the Los Angeles Police Department. Betty had just innocently stumbled upon what would soon become one of the most infamous of unsolved murders in American history; a crime that would forever be known as the "Black Dahlia Murder."

Elizabeth Short was born on July 29, 1924, in Boston, Massachusetts, to Cleo and Phoebe May Short. The third of five daughters, Elizabeth grew up in the Boston suburb of Medford. Cleo, Elizabeth's father, constructed miniature golf courses until the stock market crash of 1929. At that time, Cleo lost all of his family's life savings, and the Short family, like so many others at the time, was broke. The stress of the situation led Mr. Short to attempt the unthinkable. In 1930, Cleo's car was found abandoned on the Charleston Bridge. Authorities believed that he had committed suicide by jumping into the Charles River. Believing her husband to be dead, Phoebe May downsized herself and her five daughters into a small apartment in Medford, and began work as a bookkeeper to support the family.

Elizabeth suffered from chronic lung disease from a very young age. At fifteen, she underwent invasive lung surgery to help correct her severe chronic bronchitis and frequent asthma attacks. Elizabeth's physicians suggested she move to a milder climate, as such a move would help attenuate the young girl's symptoms. Consequently, Phoebe sent Elizabeth to live with some family friends in Miami, Florida. For the following three years, Elizabeth spent her winters in Florida, and return home for the warmer months.

In late 1942, Phoebe May received a shocking letter from her previously presumed-dead husband. In it, Cleo apologized for having abandoned his family, particularly during such a difficult time in history given the state of the Second World War. He revealed that he was now living in California. At the age of eighteen, Elizabeth moved to Vallejo to live with her father, who she hadn't seen in twelve years. This living arrangement brought some apparent contention, as an argument between the two resulted in Elizabeth moving out in January, 1943.

Youth, beauty, and sparse responsibility gave Elizabeth the ability to pursue her dream as a film star. In July of 1946, Elizabeth relocated to Los Angeles. As with many young ladies pursuing stardom in 1940s Hollywood, Elizabeth was as ambitious as she was naïve. Among her closest friends, Elizabeth was known to have more than a few boyfriends at any given time. Perhaps well aware of her delicate beauty, Elizabeth was no stranger to men who, she believed, would treat her like the queen she was. Amongst Elizabeth's string of relationships was Robert "Red" Manley, a married, twenty-five-year-old salesman. In the end, Manley was one of the last people to ever see Elizabeth Short alive.

On January 9, 1947, after a brief trip to San Diego, away from the many prying eyes around Los Angeles (LA), Elizabeth asked Manley to drop her off at the Biltmore Hotel, where she was going to meet with her sister who was visiting from Boston. Some of the hotel staff recalled seeing Elizabeth using the lobby telephone. Just a few hours later, patrons of the Crown Grill Cocktail Lounge saw Elizabeth, less than half a mile away from the Biltmore. Shortly thereafter, Elizabeth disappeared until the morning of January 15, when she was discovered by Ms. Bersinger.

An autopsy conducted on January 16, 1947, by Fredrick Newbarr, the LA County coroner at the time, revealed that the victim was five-feet five-inches, weighed approximately 115 lbs., had light blue eyes, brown hair, and badly decayed teeth. Further examination revealed ligature marks on her ankles, wrists, and neck. Much of the victim's right breast tissue had been removed, and more superficial lacerations were located on her right forearm, left upper arm, left upper side of her chest, near the mid-axillary line. Perhaps the most shocking of all the victim's mutilations was the separation of her torso from her legs, known medically as a hemicorporectomy.

Taught in the 1930s, a hemicorporectomy involves separating the lower half of the body via transection of the lumbar spine between the second and third lumbar vertebrae. The intestines are severed at the duodenum, located at the junction of the stomach and small intestines. The coroner's report also made a mention of ecchymosis, or bruising, along the incision line, suggesting that the hemicorporectomy had been performed after death. Regardless of when the operation was performed, however, a hemicorporectomy is no small task. When cutting through a human body, there are varying layers of fascia, epithelial tissue, fat, muscle, bone, cartilage, and internal organs to consider. While the apparent brutality of the crime sounds haphazard, there is a true level of skill required to perform such an extensive operation. One thing was absolutely certain; whoever had committed the murder almost certainly had a working knowledge of human anatomy as well as formal and extensive surgical training.

INTELLIGENT AND IMMORAL

George Hodel Jr. was born on October 10, 1907, in Los Angeles, to George Sr. and Esther Hodel. The only child, George Jr. was a particularly bright young boy. Noticing that their son was special, George's parents had his IQ, or intellectual quotient, tested. Scoring an astounding 186, the young George Jr. was statistically more intelligent than over ninety-eight percent of the world's population. As such, the Hodel's took advantage of their son's much higher-than-average intellect, and ensured his level of education matched his mental acuity. After a short while of intensive piano lessons, George became a musical prodigy, playing solo piano concerts in LA's famed Shrine Auditorium. News of the impressive boy reached the ears of notable Russian composer Sergei Rachmaninoff, who traveled to the Hodels' home to hear George play. At age fifteen, George graduated from Pasadena High School, and entered the prestigious California Institute of Technology (Caltech).

Because of his brilliance and talent, much of George's childhood was forfeited in his parents' pursuit of their son's success. Adolescence was really no different, as George was now enrolled as an undergraduate, something most young men and women don't reach until a bit later in life, given the average age of incoming college freshman of 18. Pubescence was, subsequently, far more awkward and confusing for the prodigy. Intense feelings of sexual desire and aggression were paired with a variable social ineptness stemming from minimal exposure to individuals his own age; ingredients for disaster. After one year, George was expelled from Caltech after it was learned that George Jr. had an affair with one of his professor's wife. The affair resulted in a pregnancy, which destroyed the professor's marriage.

In an attempt to make things right, George offered to help care for his child and marry the newly divorced woman with whom he had the affair. However, as George was so young (sixteen at the time), the woman refused his proposal. Perhaps another side-effect of an unusual upbringing, a result of rejection from the woman with whom he lost his virginity, or a combination of all the factors surrounding George's life, the professor's ex-wife was only one in a long list of women George pursued during his lifetime.

In 1928, George entered a common-law marriage with a young woman by the name of Emilia, and had a son by her, Duncan. Sometime during the 1930s, while still involved with Emilia, George legally married a model from San Francisco by the name of Dorothy Anthony, with whom he had a daughter, Tamar. The originally awkward adolescent boy who had been forced to leave university had now developed a charm and charisma to supplement his sexual desires. With almost hypnotic domination, George persuaded Emilia to allow Dorothy Anthony and Tamar to move in with them. Like a polygamist family featured on a modern reality television show, George had his proverbial cake, and was seemingly able to eat it too.

George returned to school and, in 1932, graduated from Berkley with a pre-medical degree. Immediately afterward, George Hodel enrolled in the University of California, San Francisco's (UCSF) medical program, and received his medical degree in 1936. As was the case throughout his childhood, George stood-out as a young medical resident. His hand-eye coordination, ability of perfect recall, and keen sense of the human body made

George an invaluable asset to each and every surgeon he studied under. George excelled in everything he did, enjoying a very successful life practicing medicine and, eventually, becoming the head of the LA's Social Hygiene Bureau (SHB). The Social Hygiene Bureau was developed as an attempt to help control the spread of venereal disease in LA. To say the least, the actions taken by the SHB were less than ethical. Forced sterilizations were conducted on criminals to help quell the spread of gonorrhea, syphilis, herpes, chlamydia, and a myriad of other known sexually transmitted infections. It is perhaps at this point in George's life that the final remaining residue of his moral compass was wholly eroded.

During the 1940s, similar to the situation today, Hollywood elites enjoyed lavished dinner parties and other social engagements. As the head of the SHB, George was introduced to a wide array of Hollywood heavy hitters, striking up a friendship with famed photographer Man Ray and film director John Huston. George became enthralled by the darker realms associated with surrealism. A strong proponent of the philosophy of Marquis de Sade, Dr. Hodel became progressively more interested in sadism and masochism. George's sexual desires quickly evolved to include physical dominance, humiliation, and torture. Man Ray and John Huston shared Hodel's sadomasochist philosophy and, together, the men enjoyed partying, drinking, and womanizing.

In 1940, Hodel married yet another woman, the second with whom he was legally married, John Huston's ex-wife, Dorothy Harvey. In order to reduce confusion with his other wife, Dorothy Anthony, Hodel often referred to Dorothy Harvey as "Dorero." There is another aspect of this unusual nickname that is worth noting, however. "Dorero" was meant as a dark, inside joke among his close group of friends; a combination of the Latin roots for "gift" and "sex." Because of Dr. Hodel's selfish and perverted sexual aggression, George had very little respect for women. In fact, it is safe to assume that George, much like the French philosopher Marquis de Sade whom sadism was named after, saw others as mere objects; tools to achieve his own desires, rather than fellow humans themselves.

After his tenure with the SHB, Hodel opened the First Street Clinic. In continuation of the Social Hygiene Bureau's questionable activities, George's practice fell far short of the ethical standards, which should be held by any and all medical practices. Hodel's connection to the

Hollywood elite made his First Street Clinic quite popular among movie stars, directors, producers, politicians, and many other socialites. George was more than happy to conduct operations, treatments, and exams with the utmost secrecy and discretion. At the time, abortions were illegal in the state of California. However, the laws of man seldom, if ever, got in the way of Dr. Hodel. Frequently, a married politician would bring his mistress to the First Street Clinic to, well, eliminate pregnancies and, thus, eliminate the ultimate evidence of the affair.

Dr. Hodel did little in his life out of selflessness. Though the Hollywood elite enjoyed his clinic's discretion and effective results, George was certainly getting much out of the relationships with his patients himself. As a secretive and unhinged medical doctor, Hodel was able to charge his patients as much as he wanted to. Knowing they had no other options, his patients almost always paid. Also, despite Hodel's discretion, George maintained very detailed medical records of all his patients; lest any disgruntled patient decided to turn on him.

Ruth Spaulding, George's personal secretary and mistress, was well aware of her boyfriend/boss's unethical and illegal activities. Lacking the sociopathy of her employer, Ruth was troubled with a pitting sense of guilt. On one occasion, an angry female patient approached Ms. Spaulding. Dr. Hodel, without performing the proper diagnostic testing, had diagnosed the woman with a sexually transmitted bacterial disease, and prescribed antibiotics. The woman was charged $75, the approximate equivalent of more than $1,000 today. Had the diagnosis and treatment been appropriate, the young woman would've likely accepted the bill at face value. A consult with another physician revealed that she had, in fact, been swindled. Ruth buckled under the stress of her complicit involvement in the obvious scam, and broke down to the patient. George was furious with Spaulding, noticing Ruth as an obvious threat to his empire. Shortly after this incident, in May 1945, Ruth Spaulding was found dead of barbiturate overdose. Though it is unclear whether Ruth had in fact committed suicide, there is no doubt that George was either directly or indirectly responsible for her death. The only way Ms. Spaulding could've gotten a hold of barbiturates, particularly enough to overdose with, would've come from Dr. Hodel. Not to mention the overwhelming motive George would've had to remove Ruth from his business and life.

In 1945, Hodel purchased the Sowden house, a home designed by Lloyd Wright, son of the notable American architect Frank Lloyd Wright. Effectively living as a polygamist, George lived at the Sowden property with "Dorero," their three children together, Dorothy Anthony, their daughter Tamar, and Emilia (by this time, Duncan was an independent adult).

CONNECTING THE DOTS

Known posthumously as the Black Dahlia because of her dark-colored hair, pale skin, and delicate beauty, Elizabeth Short's many male companions were often the subject of conversation between Elizabeth and her closest friends. As detectives began to investigate the mysterious murder of the Black Dahlia, officers interviewed several of Elizabeth's friends. Although they were aware of the identity of Elizabeth's salesman boyfriend "Red" Manley, they noted that Elizabeth was dating another man, whose identity was never indicated. The mystery man was certainly at the top of the investigators' list of suspects. The problem, of course, is that detectives were no closer to identifying the murderer.

A short time before her murder, it had been reported, but not corroborated, Elizabeth approached a police officer with concerns that her boyfriend had threatened to kill her, as he had recently learned that she was cheating on him. A new clue was also introduced through this anecdote; Elizabeth noted that her boyfriend was a serviceman.

Retired Los Angeles Police Department (LAPD) detective and son of George Hodel Jr., Steve Hodel, rummaged through his father's belongings after his death on May 16, 1999. Although Dr. Hodel's wishes were that all his belongings be destroyed upon his death, Steve noticed a photo album. As the former detective flipped through the pages of his late dad's album, an interesting photo captured his attention; a portrait of a young, pale woman with dark brown hair, posed in a suggestive manner. For decades following the original Black Dahlia investigation, every rookie at the LAPD the legendary unsolved murder well. Photographs of Elizabeth Short were the subject of multiple briefings, and thus, imprinted within the minds of everyone at LAPD. At that moment, as Steve Hodel looked at the portrait of this young woman, he realized that his father, for some reason, had a photograph of Elizabeth Short.

Curiosity quickly evolved into suspicion. At a point in Dr. Hodel's professional life, he volunteered to offer his medical expertise to the United States military. Through the military, George Hodel was sent all over the world. George took advantage of his newfound military experience and uniform to compliment his habit of womanizing. Thusly, Hodel often described himself as a serviceman and physician. Furthermore, Hodel's past of aggressive sadomasochism and sexual assault made him a particularly promising suspect in the Black Dahlia case. In fact, in 1950, the LAPD began to surveil Dr. Hodel as a prime suspect in the Black Dahlia case. Detectives at the time asked George to come down to the police station to answer some questions. Hodel was confident that the police had little to no evidence to connect him to the murder, and gladly accepted the officers' request. The interview was only a ruse, however. Technicians quickly flocked to the Hodel residence, installing microphones to capture every conversation within the home.

Transcripts from Dr. Hodel's surveillance are bone chilling...

◉ February 18, 1950

> ▸ 7:35 P.M. "Conversation between two men. Recorded. Hodel and man with German accent had a long conversation; following bits of conversation, however, we overheard Hodel tell the German: 'This is the best pay off I've seen between Law Enforcement Agencies. You do not have the right connections made.' Hodel states, 'I'd like to get a connection made in the D.A.'s office.' General conversation between the two: 'Any imperfections will be found. They will have to be made perfect. Don't confess ever. Two and two is not four.' Much laughter. 'We're just a couple of smart boys.' More laughter. Hodel then, in exact detail, explained to the German about his wife being stopped on Wednesday morning by McGrath and Morgan of the District Attorney's office when they [intersected] her going up her steps to the house on Franklin. It should be noted that every question asked of Mrs. Hodel was repeated verbatim by Hodel to this German. He then began to explain to the German

about his recent trial, making statements that 'They're out to get me. Two men in the D.A.'s office were transferred and demoted because of my trial.' Hodel then explained about his being questioned at the D.A.'s office on Wednesday morning, and told in great detail as to questions propounded to him at that time. One statement made to the German was as follows: 'Supposin' I did kill the Black Dahlia, they couldn't prove it now. They can't talk to my secretary anymore because she's dead [referencing Ruth Spaulding's death].' As stated, heretofore, conversation was garbled, and it was difficult to maintain a line of continuity of conversation. Hodel also referred to a woman in Camarillo. Conversation also referred to communist. One point of the conversation also said, 'Have you heard from Powers?' The man with the German accent then asked Hodel something about smoking. Hodel said, 'I can't afford it, don't smoke.' The German said, 'I can get it for you.' 'Does the name Hernandez mean anything to you?' Hodel then talked to the German about a furniture store on East 5th Street, where the cops come in and buy lingerie for $20to $50. There was much laughter at this point."

▸ 7:45 P.M. "Hodel talking to a man with an accent, possibly German [same man as before]. 'Telephone men were here. Operator? Realized there was nothing I could do, put a pillow over her head, and cover her with a blanket. Get a taxi. Call Georgia Street Receiving Hospital right away. Expired at 12:39. They thought there was something fishy. Anyway, now they may have figured it out. Killed her. Maybe, I did kill my secretary. They must have enough on him to be guilty or he wouldn't have confessed. Time for research (lots of pounding). FBI were here to see me too, three weeks ago.'"

▸ 8:20 P.M. "Sounded as though the two men went down steps and entered the basement and began digging. Something was referred to 'Not a trace.' It also appeared as though a pipe was being hit."

▸ 8:25 P.M. "Woman screamed."

▸ 8:27 P.M. "Woman screamed again. It should be noted that a woman was not heard before the time of screaming since 6:50 p.m. She was not in any conversation, and not heard of again until the time of letting out these two screams."

Who was the mysterious woman whose screams appeared at 8:25 p.m.? Is it possible that Dr. Hodel and his German guest had committed yet another murder? Had George just admitted to murdering his former secretary, Ruth Spaulding? Did he just admit to killing Elizabeth Short as well?

Despite the overwhelming evidence implicating George Hodel in these cases, he was never tried for his crimes. There have been many speculations that Dr. Hodel's powerful ties to the Hollywood elite made him more or less untouchable; immunity guaranteed by a vast collection of explicit and impeccably detailed medical records. In 1950, Hodel ran off to Hawaii, a U.S. territory at the time, and married an upper-class Filipino woman by the name of Hortensia Laguda. Four children later, Hortensia and George divorced in the 1960s. Hodel returned to the United States in 1990 and married (legally) for the fourth and final time to a woman named June. Until his death in 1999, George and June lived in an apartment in Oakland, California. It is likely no coincidence that their apartment overlooked Mountain View Cemetery, Elizabeth Short's final resting place.

While it's difficult to pinpoint George Hodel as the true murderer in the Black Dahlia case, his story strongly implicates his guilt. At fourteen-years-old, Tamar, George's daughter, accused her father of incestuous rape. Eventually, the charges against Dr. Hodel were dropped, despite witness testimony suggesting Dr. Hodel performed an abortion on his teenage daughter after accidentally impregnating her; a fact that George himself never disputed. Hodel later sexually assaulted Tamar's daughter, spiking her drink with a powerful sedative and taking suggestive photographs of his naked granddaughter while she was unconscious.

Wherever Hodel went, death followed. During the '60s, while married to Hortensia, the two spent time in the Philippines. During this time in Manila, a woman's body was found discarded on a pile of garbage, drained of blood. Like the Black Dahlia, the woman's body was separated in two at the waist. The unknown woman was regarded as the "Chop-Chop Lady," and later, identified as Lucila Lalu. It is also believed that multiple murders in Northern California during the late 1960s were committed by Dr. George Hodel.

Letters were sent to the San Francisco Police Department, taunting detectives investigating the murders. Cyphers were included to decode the suspected murderer's encoded admission letters. Because of the suspect's obsession with cryptography, the serial murder would eventually gain the moniker "Zodiac Killer." During his investigation, Steve Hodel had an independent graphologist compare the Zodiac Killer's letters with his father's handwriting. The two were determined to have been written by the same person.

Dr. George Hodel was likely the most intelligent, manipulative, malicious, and sadistic murderers in human history. Hodel lived a life of success, power, and fame, never answering for his crimes. It is possible that dozens of people died at the hands of a man obsessed with death, sex, and torture. There's solace in the fact that George Hodel is now dead. For believers in the afterlife, Hodel must now and forever answer for his crimes against humanity. Those who are skeptical of life after death can sleep well, knowing that Dr. Hodel can never hurt another human being again.

CHAPTER 2:
DR. H.H. HOLMES

AMERICA'S FIRST SERIAL KILLER

On May 7, 1896, a calm and collected man slowly walked the gallows, drawing nearer and nearer to the noose. With an audience of notable businessmen, officers and lawyers, the executioner guided the murderer's head and neck through the noose. As the criminal muttered his final remarks, the lever was pulled, releasing the platform from under one of the most infamous men in history. As the rope lengthened to a tightened clap, the criminal's neck didn't snap. Instead, the vicious murderer met a poetic end, struggling to grasp life as he strangled to death. Though Henry Howard Holmes was relatively young, his thirty-fifth birthday being only nine days away, Holmes had confessed to killing twenty-

23

seven people, and was speculated to have killed as many as 200 people in his lifetime. After his execution at Monyamensing Prison, the "Beast of Chicago" would be remembered as one of America's first serial killers.

Herman Webster Mudgett was born on May 16, 1861, to Levi Horton and Theodate Page Mudgett (née Price). At the age of sixteen, Mudgett graduated from Phillips Exeter Academy in his hometown Gilmanton, New Hampshire. In 1878, Mudgett married Clara Lovering in Alton, and had a son by her, Robert Lovering Mudgett. Mudgett went on to attend the University of Vermont in Burlington at eighteen years old. After one year, Mudgett left the university, citing dissatisfaction with the school. In 1882, Mudgett continued his studies at the University of Michigan's Department of Medicine and Surgery and graduated in the June of 1884. Mudgett demonstrated an impressive aptitude for surgery, working closely with the chief anatomy instructor while in college. He would go on to pursue an apprenticeship with Nahum Wight, a massive advocate of human dissection at the time.

Mudgett was clever, narcissistic, and extremely driven by the desire to achieve wealth and fame. Unfortunately, the confluence of these traits would guide

Mudgett into a realm of confidence trickery and, eventually, serial murder. Years after graduating medical school, Mudgett refuted murder claims, citing that he was nothing more than an insurance fraudster. Not that the latter was benevolent by any measure, but drew far less consequence when compared to murder. Mudgett's disregard for the human body was rooted in his earlier insurance fraud. While in medical school, Mudgett admittedly used cadavers as proof of bodies to collect life insurance. This was done on multiple occasions and, during this time, it is believed that Mudgett defrauded today's equivalent of millions of dollars from life insurance companies.

As with most con men, Mudgett quickly realized that his name and fraudulent history would make him an easy target of guilt, whether he was truly innocent or not. In the 1880s, Mudgett moved to Mooers Folk, New York. Shortly after, a rumor spread that a young boy was seen with Mudgett before his disappearance, making Mudgett a prime suspect. It is still unknown whether Mudgett was involved in the child's disappearance. A formal investigation was never opened, and Mudgett quickly left town.

In Philadelphia, Pennsylvania, Mudgett landed a job as keeper at Norristown State Hospital. This stint was very short-lived, as Mudgett left after only a few days. Mudgett soon began work at a drugstore in Philadelphia, but since a child had died after taking medicine formulated at the pharmacy, Mudgett vehemently denied having anything to do with the child's death and, as before, promptly left the city.

Mudgett decided to move further West, to avoid any association with the scams and scandals of the Eastern Seaboard. It was at this point, before making his final move to Chicago, that Mudgett decided to change his name to Henry Howard Holmes–a further attempt to quell the loudly roaring past from New York and Pennsylvania.

In August 1886, Holmes arrived in Chicago, and met a drugstore owner by the name of Dr. Elizabeth S. Holton. Holton saw Holmes' promise, and gave him a job at her store. Holmes proved to be an incredibly hard worker, eventually purchasing the store from Dr. Holton the same year. The drugstore became increasingly more profitable and successful under Dr. Holmes' management. Holmes had collected enough capital to expand his empire, centering his focus on a vacant lot across from his drugstore on 63rd Street.

THE MURDER CASTLE

Holmes purchased the empty lot positioned directly across the street from his drugstore. Construction began in 1887 for a planned two-story, mixed-use building containing apartments on the second floor, and retail spaces as well as a new drugstore on the first. After Holmes refused to pay architects and the steel company supplying the materials for the building's construction, a lawsuit was filled in 1888. Despite the overwhelming obstacles standing in the way of Holmes' dream pavilion, like so many scam artists in the past, present, and future, Holmes simply continued to lie and defraud. In 1892, Holmes told investors that he planned to construct a third floor on the building, which he intended as hotel space for the upcoming World's Columbian Exposition (Chicago's World Fair of 1893). The hotel portion was never completed, but its concept secured Holmes even more financial backing as he needed to proverbially continue to rob Peter to pay Paul.

Though the building would never be completed, the persistently under-construction project would come to be known as the infamous "Murder Castle." Like something out of a modern horror film, Dr. Holmes had a series of soundproofed secret rooms, passages, mazes, and hallways; many of which seemingly led to nowhere. Later investigations would reveal a collection of chutes that would lead straight down to the building's basement, where Dr. Holmes stored vats of acid, calcium oxide (quicklime), and a crematorium; none of which were even remotely appropriate for Dr. Holmes' proposed intention for the building.

Julia Smythe, her husband, Ned Connor, and their daughter, Pearl, moved into Holmes' building toward the end of the 1880s. Julia worked at the jewelry counter in Holmes' pharmacy. During this time, Holmes began sleeping with Ms. Smythe. After learning of the affair, Connor moved away, leaving his wife and daughter. Julia obtained custody of Pearl, and the two remained at Holmes' building, where Julia continued her relationship with Holmes. On Christmas Eve of 1891, Julia and Pearl went missing. After Holmes' eventual arrest a few years later, he claimed that Julia had perished during a botched abortion, though reference to Pearl's fate was never made. What truly happened to Julia and Pearl is still a mystery, but it is very likely that they were amongst Holmes' first murder victims.

In May 1892, Emeline Cigrande began working in Holmes' building. Another of Dr. Holmes' paramours, Emeline went missing that December. Around the same time, another young woman, Edna Van Tassel, vanished while staying at Holmes' building. It is widely accepted amongst experts that, as serial murderers graduate from their first human killing, their murder rate accelerates. This is true of many of history's most notorious serial killers, and appears to have rung true in the case of Dr. Holmes. Each killing became exponentially easier than the last. Not to mention, earlier in Holmes' life, he demonstrated a blatant disregard of human corpses when committing fraud. He didn't need to travel far to maintain the same level of disrespect for the living.

During a short stint at the Chemical Bank on Dearborn Street, Holmes became acquainted with an ex-convict and carpenter named Benjamin Pitezel. The two quickly became thick-as-thieves, as it were. Pitezel was Holmes' associate for several criminal schemes. Later, a Chicago district attorney referred to Pitezel as "Holmes' tool ... his creature."

In 1893, a minimally successful, one-time actress, Minnie Williams, moved to Chicago. Holmes later claimed to have met Ms. Williams at an employment office, where he offered her a job as his personal stenographer. Williams first fell victim to Holmes' trickery, agreeing to transfer the deed to a property she owned in Fort Worth, Texas, to a man by the name of Alexander Bond (one of Holmes' many aliases). The deed was officially transferred in April 1893. The next month, Holmes and Williams posed as husband and wife, renting an apartment in Chicago's Lincoln Park. A month later, Minnie's sister, Annie, came to visit. In July, Annie wrote to her aunt that she was to accompany a man referred to as "Brother Harry" to Europe. Annie and Minnie were never seen again after July 5, 1893.

In addition to his evil nature, Holmes had quite the entrepreneurial spirit. Using his medical knowledge and connections with the healthcare community, Holmes began to sell human skeletons to medical schools and laboratories. Holmes made an impressive profit from his skeleton sales, as the remains didn't cost him a cent. He, and occasionally, a hired assistant, would surgically remove all the flesh from the skeletons of Holmes' murder victims.

The remains were then tossed into vats of acid and lime to effectively eliminate the last shred of evidence.

Like so many times before, Holmes fled Chicago in July 1894, after insurance companies attempted to prosecute Holmes for arson and insurance fraud. He reappeared in Fort Worth where he had inherited property from the Williams sisters. On the property, Holmes intended to build another "castle," similar to his previous venture in Chicago.

SCAM GONE SIDEWAYS

In one of Holmes' many scams, he was able to convince his trusted sidekick, Pitezel, to fake his death. As yet another life insurance fraud scheme, Pitezel's wife could collect $10,000 of life insurance, which she was to split with Holmes and Holmes' trusted attorney, Jeptha Howe. The scheme was planned to take place in Philadelphia, and Holmes was tasked with locating a cadaver to pose as Pitezel. The plan was conducted much like a fine-tuned play. Pitezel was going to play the part of an inventor by the name of B.F. Hunter, who would tragically die and become severely disfigured in a lab explosion (the disfigurement was necessary, as the cadaver would likely not look like Pitezel).

Holmes, however, had a different idea. Later, during trial, Holmes admitted to using chloroform (a common general anesthetic of the time). Holmes rendered Pitezel unconscious and set his body on fire with the accelerant benzene. Forensic evidence presented at trial, however, proved that Holmes had, in fact, used chloroform on the already dead Pitezel. This was likely done in an attempt to retroactively implicate suicide, thus exonerating Holmes should he ever be charged with murder.

Dr. Holmes, on the basis of Pitezel's genuine corpse, collected the payout from the life insurance company. He then proceeded to manipulate Pitezel's widow to give him custody of three of her five children, Nellie, Alice, and Howard. The eldest and youngest remained with their mother. Holmes then traveled throughout North America with the three children. Holmes later admitted to killing two of the children, Nellie and Alice, by forcing them into a trunk, locking it, drilling a hole at the top of the trunk, and feeding a small tube through the hole. Holmes then attached the other end of the tube to a gas line. After asphyxiating the girls until they stopped making noise,

Holmes buried their nude bodies in the cellar of a rental property in Toronto. A Philadelphia police detective, Frank Geyer, later discovered the decomposed bodies of the Pitezel girls in the Toronto home.

Holmes' murder spree continued until his arrest on November 17, 1894. Despite being extremely elusive, Holmes had been successfully tracked and captured due to the efforts of the private Pinkerton National Detective Agency. In October 1895, Holmes faced trial for the murder of his former associate Benjamin Pitezel. A speedy trial resulted in a swift sentence of execution. By that time, it was blatantly evident that Holmes had murdered all three of the Pitezel children, although Howard's body was never found. Following his conviction, Holmes confessed to twenty-seven murders in Illinois, Indiana, and Toronto, as well as six attempted murders. Holmes confessions, however, turned out to be mostly nonsense, as several of the people he "confessed" to killing were, in fact, still alive and well.

Thus, the story ends where we began. Holmes' relatively short life met an end at the noose. There is no more fitting death for such a prolific and twisted murderer than suffering asphyxiation by rope. Like the cruelty he so brutally showed the Pitezel girls, Dr. Holmes met a violent end, hopelessly struggling to capture his breath. Though he demonstrated such calmness and stoicism immediately before he was hanged, the panic and fear he brought his victims was now his own. Clenching the tightened rope wrapped around his neck, desperateness and helplessness flooded his mind, as his heart began to beat ever faster to compensate for the diminished oxygen supply. His eyes began to press forward, almost exiting their sockets. Holmes' tongue began to fill most of his mouth, as his head's blood pressure exponentially rose. The spectators watched as the "Beast of Chicago" shook of suffocation. As quickly as it began, his feet twitched until it reached a standstill. Dr. Holmes' execution was complete. The monster was no longer among the living, and could now face judgment for bringing a plague of death to so many innocent people.

Holmes' "Murder Castle" remained standing until 1938, at which point, it was torn down. In its place, the Englewood branch of the United States Postal Service was erected shortly after and is still there today. It is believed that the land is still haunted by the many spirits of those who met an end at Holmes' vicious hands. Whether you believe this to be true or not, we can certainly all agree that the 63rd Street property carries an undoubtable eeriness and gloom; a constant reminder of a perverted, selfish, vile monster who, albeit human in form, was most definitely no less than evil incarnate.

CHAPTER 3:
TAINTED DRUGS

FRAUDULENT PRESCRIPTIONS

B arry Cadden graduated from the University of Rhode Island in 1990, immediately continuing his education at the university's college of pharmacy. Upon graduating as a pharmacist, Cadden took an oath to always maintain the "welfare of humanity and relief of human suffering [as his] primary concern," as is the case with all graduates of any healthcare program. Pharmacists, like all other healthcare professionals, play an integral part in the nation's medical system. Essentially, pharmacists are the middlemen that exist between patients and the nation's drug supply. Unethical behavior can, therefore, have dire implications and extremely serious impacts.

Now that Cadden had graduated from pharmacy school, he sought to make good on his oath, opening a compounding pharmacy in 1998 called the New England Compounding Center (NECC). Unlike your local pharmacies such as Walgreens, CVS, or a smaller mom-n'-pop operation, compounding pharmacies actually formulate their drugs for patients who require personalized versions of their medication. If, for example, a patient suffered from a known allergy against an ingredient in something they had been prescribed, a compounding pharmacy may be able to formulate a customized drug, excluding the ingredient that the patient is allergic to.

Cadden's entrepreneurial spirit drove him to dream big. Instead of exclusively selling drugs in Framingham, Massachusetts, where the NECC was based, Cadden wanted to sell and distribute his products to hospitals and clinics throughout the United States. In alignment with this dream, Cadden had each of his sales meetings recorded, so that his traveling salesmen and saleswomen could repeatedly listen to his instructions while on the road. In one recorded session, Cadden is heard discussing the characteristics that separate the NECC from its competitors. He makes reference to the NECC lab's cleanliness, sterility, and fine-tuned drug-making protocols. Essentially, Cadden wanted his sales team to focus on his company's quality products.

However, Barry Cadden had one significant problem–government regulation.

If the NECC were to sell drugs in bulk, like large-scale manufacturers Pfizer or Bayer, Cadden's business would receive obligatory Food and Drug Administration oversight. But, if Cadden were to call his business a pharmacy, filling customized prescriptions for individual patients, the NECC would fall no further than the jurisdiction of the Massachusetts State Board of Pharmacy; precisely what Barry wanted.

The Massachusetts State Board of Pharmacy had three inspectors for more than a thousand pharmacies in Massachusetts. These inspectors had minimal, if any, experience with clean-rooms, as well as minor knowledge of the guidelines for compounding. This was exactly the type of oversight and regulation Cadden preferred–none at all. In another recording of one of Cadden's sales meetings, Cadden revealed how little he thought of the state's board of pharmacy, referencing the apparent cluelessness the inspectors demonstrate when touring the NECC facility.

In order for Cadden to receive such little regulation, he would require prescriptions to justify exemption from FDA regulation. The NECC, therefore, asked for their customers, in this case hospitals and clinics, to provide them with a list of patient names with their orders. Cadden would then have a collection of employees who would take these orders and patient names, and type up prescriptions to match the drugs being sent to the medical facilities.

Obviously, everyone working at the NECC and its customers knew that the patient names didn't matter. Therefore, in addition to legitimate patients' names, the NECC's in-house team would also write fake prescriptions with doctors' names, nurses' names, even the names of historical figures, celebrities, and fictional characters. Later, investigations revealed prescriptions written for "Chester Cheeto," "Calvin Klein," "Filet O'Fish," "Donald Trump" and "Big Baby Jesus," to name a few.

In another sales meeting recording, a salesmen inquires about the fake prescriptions. Cadden quickly dismisses the question, acknowledging that the fake prescriptions are "one of the more difficult things we [the NECC] do." Cadden also makes a comment about how "that" discussion is "for another time" when they're not being recorded. While most would rightly consider the NECC's actions as fraud, Cadden saw his company's unethical behavior as a promising business plan.

Those afflicted with narcissism and greed are markedly capable of lying and manipulating others. However, the most significant deception is that of themselves. From an evolutionary standpoint, it is believed that self-deception originated as an ability to better facilitate interpersonal manipulation. In an article titled, "The evolution and psychology of self-deception," William von Hippel and Robert Trivers argue that self-deception evolved to aid in the masking of obvious cues that might reveal an individual's deceptive intent. In other words, if we believe the lies we tell, our lies become eerily indistinguishable from truth. In Barry Cadden's case, he believed that his actions were generally innocuous and victimless. The NECC, with Cadden at the helm, exploited loopholes and shortcuts to avoid FDA regulation. Undoubtedly unethical and inarguably illegal, Cadden was able to convince himself, as well as his employees, that the NECC was simply behaving in a way that was savvy, taking advantage of preexisting flaws in the system. In his mind, Cadden wasn't committing fraud, he was just being clever.

Cadden's attempts to evade FDA regulation were actually quite successful. In 2006, after the FDA decided to investigate complaints of the quality of the NECC's

41

pharmaceutical products, Cadden received a warning letter. While this might seem like the beginning of the end of Cadden's scheme, he quickly countered with an argument of jurisdiction. In a response letter to the FDA's warning, Cadden writes: "The NECC does not process or repackage approved drugs in a manner that would subject us [the NECC] to FDA regulation." Essentially, because the NECC was producing medications for individual patients, the FDA had no business questioning the NECC's methods and quality of its products. At this, the FDA stood down and Cadden's company continued to grow.

In 2011, a national drug shortage created an ideal environment for the NECC to expand at an astonishingly rapid rate. Anyone with an elementary knowledge of economics could see that the decrease in supply provided a marked increase in demand. To meet the newfound inflation of demand, Cadden ramped up the NECC's production to help supplement the nation's drug supply. NECC employees are asked to work overtime to produce overwhelmingly large quantities of drugs in high demand. Understandably, Cadden's business began to skyrocket.

Despite the NECC's fraudulent prescription fabrication, there was something far more sinister occurring in the background. The NECC was sued in 2004 by a woman whose husband had died after receiving a steroid injection, Depomedrol, formulated at the NECC. In a swift attempt to conceal the blemish on the NECC's record, the NECC quickly settled the suit, without admission of wrongdoing, for $400,000. Although this suit was an opportunity for Cadden to learn and improve the operations of the NECC, this would unfortunately be one of many cases to result from Barry Cadden's unethical and irresponsible leadership of the NECC.

MYSTERIOUS MENINGITIS OUTBREAK

A couple of hours outside of Nashville, Tennessee, there rests the quant town of Albany, Kentucky. There, Eddie Lovelace spends a successful career as a lawyer, earning a sterling reputation amongst those in the close-knit, Albany community. Lovelace was described as the type of person that would gladly help anyone who asked. The dependable, trustworthy, and integrous Lovelace eventually rose to the position of circuit-court judge. Known to be kind, generous and above all else, fair, the honorable Judge Lovelace was very well respected, even by defendants whose cases were brought before the judge. A beloved community member, friend, husband, father, and grandfather, it is an understatement to say that Eddie left quite the positive impact on just about everyone who was lucky enough to know him.

In August 2012, although in good health, Lovelace traveled to a clinic in Saint Thomas Midtown Hospital in Nashville. To relieve pain and inflammation in his neck resulting from a car accident, the judge was receiving a relatively routine steroid injection in his spine. Shortly after the injection, the seventy-eight-year-old Lovelace began to suffer from acute headache. Then, as the headache became progressively worse, the judge began to complain of numbness in his fingers. Just a few days later, Eddie's condition significantly worsened. Joyce, Eddie's wife, recalls seeing her husband, with a noticeable grimace on his face. The judge proceeded to tell his wife that his "legs aren't working," and that he'd fallen twice while trying to get the paper from the front lawn.

Lovelace was taken to the Vanderbilt University Medical Center in Nashville. Eddie's symptoms were reminiscent of neural dysfunction and, as such, a doctor at the hospital suspected that Eddie must have suffered a

44

stroke. Typically, the effects of a stroke are instantaneous, and some functions can be regained in the hours, days, and weeks, following the initial episode. In the judge's case, however, his condition was continuing to worsen. After just a few days of being admitted, Lovelace became unresponsive.

As the Lovelace clan gathered around their patriarch, a few doors down from the judge's hospital room, a fifty-five-year-old man was also fighting for his life, having just received a diagnosis of meningitis. Dr. William Schaffner, one of the attending physicians at the Vanderbilt Medical Center at the time, remembers the unusual circumstances surrounding the patient's diagnosis. In an attempt to confirm the diagnosis, the medical team sent samples to Vanderbilt's in-house laboratory. There, technicians could grow the pathogen, identify it, and determine the proper course of treatment to cure the patient's disease. However, the lab was unsuccessful in growing the pathogen infecting the patient's meninges and, subsequently, could not identify the bacterial causative agent.

In a "Hail Mary" attempt to get to the bottom of this mysterious case of meningitis, a physician decided to send yet another sample, this time to test for the presence of fungus. When the results come back positive, the medical team knew they were, in fact, dealing with fungal meningitis; a very deadly form of the disease, but also quite rare.

The central nervous system is extremely well protected, with multiple layers existing between sensitive nervous tissue and the internal environment of the human body. The external environment is even further separated from nervous tissue by layers of bone, muscle, fat, skin, as well as the body's immune system. While bacteria and viruses are occasionally capable of surpassing all these degrees of protection, fungi are less likely to evade these mechanisms. In fact, fungal meningitis is most likely a result of direct contamination of cerebrospinal fluid by a fungal spore.

In relatively uncharted territory, physicians scrambled to understand the source of the fungal infection. They would later find that this second patient had recently received a steroid injection at the same clinic where Eddie Lovelace had received an injection in his neck. Placing the puzzle pieces together, healthcare workers at Vanderbilt contacted the clinic to trace the origin of the apparent common denominator. Both Lovelace and the other patient had received steroid injections formulated and provided by the NECC.

NOT SUCH A FUNGI

T he common adage of past behavior as predictive of future behavior held true for Barry Cadden. As was the case with the initial suit brought against the NECC as well as the FDA's warning letter, Cadden's response to any allegation of NECC's wrongdoing was swiftly met with argument and "proof."

Whenever a lot, or batch, of a particular drug is formulated, particularly those meant to be sterile for injection, must be subject to an independent evaluation of the product's sterility. To do this, a lab receives a set of samples from the batch of the respective drug, and attempts to grow possible contaminants on a wide range of different mediums. Basically, the independent lab provides an ideal environment for just about anything to grow in their lab. Thus, if a batch of drugs were contaminated, the lab would be able to identify microbial growth after only a few days.

A report provided by Cadden demonstrated that the batch of methylprednisolone acetate (MPA) in question was, in fact, found to be sterile. The report by the independent laboratory verified that, after fourteen days, no microbes were identified. While superficially, this report appears to contradict the suspicions that the NECC's steroid injections were contaminated, there is a scientific explanation for the lab's result.

Instead of providing the laboratory with the standard twenty samples per batch of drug manufactured, the NECC was sending only one. Furthermore, this one sample was no more than 5 milliliters in volume. For perspective, this particular batch was about 12.5 liters. The probability of capturing a contaminant, particularly a fungus, in what is essentially 0.04% of the total batch is minuscule; the best real-world example of finding a proverbial needle in a very large haystack.

Once again, the NECC, under Cadden's leadership, was choosing to substitute fact with fraud. While the concoction of fake prescriptions was wrong, and very illegal, the true impact on individual patients was, to be fair, quite small. As Cadden fell deeper and deeper into his misconstrued perception of business, however, the NECC's unethical activities began to spread into just about everything they did, like a cancer.

It is believed that humans can become progressively more deceptive through time. The underlying theory of this phenomenon argues that, much like our response to abuse, the emotional centers in our brain can be desensitized by deception. In other words, imagine a small, seemingly insignificant lie. Usually, when we tell an occasional lie, we experience a catecholamine storm–norepinephrine and epinephrine surge throughout our circulation, causing increased heart rate, breathing rate, and even perspiration (sweating). These physiological responses rest at the foundation of "lie-detector," or polygraph, tests. However, as lying becomes more frequent and borders on the pathological, these physiological responses begin to diminish, especially if the person has become increasingly self-deceptive.

In 2012, over 798 people had contracted fungal meningitis, and over 100 deaths. Cadden's choice to evade regulation and oversight only served to minimize the NECC's accountability. Six years later, in 2018, Barry Cadden and Glen Chin, a pharmacist that worked at the NECC to maintain quality control, were charged with eleven counts of second-degree murder. Cadden was sentenced to nine years in federal prison, and Chin was sentenced to eight years.

Although the NECC had been dissolved, and those responsible for the illness and deaths of so many patients were punished, the families impacted by the NECC's and Cadden's dishonesty and fraudulence will forever feel the theft Cadden committed. Likely wishing Cadden had broken into their homes and taken every last material possession they had, Cadden stole the one irreplaceable thing these family's had, their loved ones.

Eddie Lovelace passed away on September 27, 2012. His family and community will remember Judge Lovelace as the kind, jovial, and incomparably integrous person he was. There is a sad and almost poetic irony in the unfortunate circumstances relating to Lovelace's death; a fair, honest, hard-working man killed by the actions of a person who was the antithesis of all of the above. Barry Cadden may not have consciously intended to harm the patients affected by his selfish negligence. Nevertheless, his actions did, in fact, damage the lives of so many.

Every last action we make can have monumental effects on any number of things down the line. In the case of the NECC, a series of "white lies" quickly darkened to result in a hundred deaths. Healthcare professionals should uphold their commitments, and avoid deviation at all costs. The resulting consequences could be fatal. Unfortunately, human nature exists within us all–businessmen, medical professionals, bankers, even bag-boys at the grocery store. Hence, the immense importance of regulation and oversight. Standards are in place to ensure the safety of patients. Is it annoying to constantly have to answer to an agency or institution like the FDA? It certainly can be frustrating. But, in all things we do, we must be held accountable, lest our animal nature to take "the path of least resistance" takeover.

CHAPTER 4:
IMAGINARY CANCER

A BOOMING CAREER

Farid Fata, born in Lebanon, moved to the United States in the 1990s, receiving a prestigious fellowship at the distinguished Sloan Kettering cancer center in New York. Because of his impressive training, Dr. Fata gained a sterling reputation as an expert in the field of oncology. So much so, in fact, that Dr. Fata's clinics in suburban Detroit had immense waitlists for patient consultations that took minutes. From 2005 to 2013, Fata built his practice, employing over sixty employees in seven different offices. During this time, it is reported that Dr. Fata was seeing over 17,000 patients. To put things in perspective, if Dr. Farid Fata saw all of these patients in a year, and assuming he worked every weekday in the year (without exception) from 9:00 a.m. to 5:00 p.m., he would've only been able to spend an average of seven minutes with each of his patients. In a 2018 survey of U.S. oncologists, over ninety percent of oncologists reported spending more than twice the time Dr. Fata was spending with his patients. Even so, it is widely acknowledged that oncologists need to spend even longer with their patients. What made Dr. Fata so special? His practice was booming. Farid Fata was, at this point, the largest provider of oncology treatment in the state of Michigan. Colleagues of Dr. Fata's would refer their own family members to be cared for by the reputable physician.

A majority of Fata's practice involved the use of expensive chemotherapy treatments. Known broadly as antineoplastics, chemotherapeutic agents have a myriad of different mechanisms of action. Generally, however, all antineoplastics share a common result–to stop and destroy cancer cells. Unlike the treatment of bacterial, viral, fungal, or other parasitic infections, chemotherapeutics tend not to be specific to cancer cells, and indiscriminately damage cells throughout the patient's body. The subsequent side effects of antineoplastics can be severe. However, as the remedy is often better than the disease itself; physicians and patients are willing to accept the trade-off of, hopefully, momentary discomfort for long-term remission.

That being said, chemotherapy is an arduous journey that should not be taken in haste. If a patient presents to a clinic with symptoms resembling strep throat, a physician may decide to prescribe an antibiotic without verifying the diagnosis with a rapid strep test. While there is contention whether or not this is good practice, an antibiotic is unlikely to cause any harm to the patient (unless, of course, they're allergic to the respective drug). For cancer, however, the treatment can have lasting effects on a patient. Some antineoplastics are even known to cause secondary cancers. Therefore, the burden rests on the physician to get their diagnosis right. This sort of "due diligence," if you will, assumes a physician who is bound to his ethical obligations to their patients. As we will see in Dr. Fata's case, greed can readily clout the judgment of even the most reputable of physicians.

CHEMO TO CASH

Farid Fata was often regarded as having a comforting and kind bedside manner; that was, however, until you questioned his diagnosis and treatment. Fata would threaten patients that, without him, they would die. When Fata's patients, often feeling pressured by the doctor, agreed to take the chemotherapeutic regiment prescribed, Dr. Fata would bill the patients' insurance companies thousands of dollars per treatment. In a short time, Farid Fata became the top biller of Medicare in the nation. Throughout his career, Fata billed BlueCross and Medicare a total of over $500,000,000. While what Fata billed these insurance companies and what he personally received were not the same, he is still doing more than alright for himself. From 2007 to 2013, Dr. Fata is said to have received more than $91 million in reimbursements from Medicare alone. Fata quickly had over $17 million on hand, not including the value of his ever-growing empire of oncology practices named Michigan Hematology and Oncology (MHO). Dr. Fata lived with his wife and three children in a $1.5 million, 6,000 square-foot mansion. He also owned property in his original home of Lebanon, and reportedly considered purchasing a castle there too.

In 2010, an experienced oncology nurse, Angela Swantek, began to notice that Dr. Fata's methods were peculiar, to say the least. Swantek interviewed to become an infusion nurse at one of Fata's clinics. Ms. Swantek recalls the clinic as being very busy, which was encouraging for her. With over twenty years of experience, Swantek enjoyed keeping busy. However, on her second visit to the clinic, Swantek not only noticed that drugs were being disposed of improperly, but that, for some reason, drugs were being administered over a longer amount of time than recommended. In other words, if a particular drug was meant to be administered over a few minutes, Dr. Fata instructed that the infusion take an hour or two. That way, Dr. Fata could bill the insurance company for even more money. Noticing that this is an inappropriate and potentially dangerous practice for the patients, Swantek sent a letter of her concerns to the state of Michigan.

Although Swantek's actions were warranted, the response she received from the Michigan state medical board is far different from what anyone would have expected. A year after submitting her complaint, Swantek received a response from state authorities that there wasn't enough evidence to open an investigation regarding Dr. Fata. Unfortunately, this would prove to be a terrible mistake as Fata continued to inappropriately treat his patients.

In 2013, Dr. Fata diagnosed Monica Flagg, fifty-four years old, with multiple myeloma. Also known as Kahler's disease, multiple myeloma is characterized by the cancerous overgrowth of plasma cells, a lineage of immune cells. Because of the dramatic pervasive nature of multiple myeloma, Ms. Flagg would require a lifetime of chemotherapy treatment in order to have even a chance of survival. After her first round of chemotherapy, Flagg fractured her leg in two places. Because Fata was in Lebanon at the time, Monica consulted with another physician working at one of Fata's practices. As is protocol, Dr. Soe Maunglay performed a routine physical exam and blood panel. The results were shocking for both Maunglay and Flagg. Dr. Maunglay recalls that, just by looking at the chart, Flagg's results were inconsistent with what would be expected in an active cancer patient. Suspicious of his findings, Maunglay reviewed Fata's files on Flagg the following day. Dr. Maunglay could find nothing to justify a chemotherapy regiment. Maunglay swiftly assured Flagg that she had been misdiagnosed, suggested she take her records to another doctor immediately, and warned her never to return to Fata again.

Fata's plan for Flagg was simple—diagnose her with a cancer that would have to be treated throughout her life and, subsequently, receive insurance payouts for as long as Flagg continued treatment. Although Maunglay was set to leave MHO the following month, his discovery of the highly unethical treatment of a healthy patient with chemotherapy drove Dr. Maunglay to feel he needed to stop Fata. Even physicians, however, make occasional mistakes. Maunglay would have to find more evidence of intentional misconduct and fraud in order to take Fata down.

THE BIGGER THEY ARE

D r. Maunglay didn't have to search too hard to find glaring evidence of unethical and even illegal behavior on the part of Fata. After auditing several MHO patient records, Maunglay discovered that Fata had been administering intravenous immunoglobulin therapeutics, known as IVIG, to patients, despite no apparent medical justification for doing so. Why would Dr. Fata be administering a therapy for no good reason? Well, as appears to be the common theme with Fata's actions, money was his motivation. Weeks later, the FBI responded to a complaint made by former MHO Office Manager George Karadsheh. Karadsheh became suspicious as a growing number of physicians, nurses, and other MHO employees complained about Fata's overly aggressive chemotherapy regimens. Following up on Maunglay's discovery of inappropriate IVIG administration, Karadsheh consulted one of MHO's infusion nurses who noted that over a period of one week, thirty-eight of forty patients who didn't meet the criteria for rewiring IVIG were, in fact, receiving the immunotherapy at Dr. Fata's direction.

Because of the actions taken by Karadsheh and Maunglay, Dr. Farad Fata was arrested on August 6, 2013, by FBI agents on charges of healthcare fraud. Originally held on $170,000 bond, federal authorities were aware that Fata and his wife had over $9 million of assets that had yet to be seized. Furthermore, Fata's Lebanese citizenship made him an extreme flight risk. Thus, Fata's bond was raised to a whopping $9 million.

Throughout the process of the disgraced doctor's trial, federal investigators revealed evidence of over 553 patients Fata had either bullied or deceived into receiving overly aggressive and unnecessary chemotherapy. Investigators also identified over $34 million Fata had fraudulently charged from his patients' health insurance. Based on these appalling transgressions, United States District Attorney for the Eastern District of Michigan, Barbara McQuade, sought a twenty-three-count indictment against Fata. If convicted on all charges, Fata would be facing 175 years in prison, as well as the possibility of having his naturalization revoked, and thus, deported to Lebanon. Facing such a potentially devastating sentence, Fata plead guilty.

Despite the fact that Fata received a lesser sentence of forty-five years, he was forced to sit through and listen to a long line of witness testimonies of patients who had received inappropriate treatment from Fata. Robert Sobieray, one of Fata's patients, lost nearly all his teeth as a result of the drugs Fata had prescribed for his non-existent blood cancer. Patty Hester lost much of her hair and developed high blood pressure after being falsely diagnosed with, and subsequently treated, for terminal myelodysplastic syndrome. These are two of potentially thousands of patients harmed as a result of the actions taken by an unethical, greedy, selfish, immoral, and entirely despicable former physician.

If there is a lesson that can be learned from Dr. Fata's shameful behavior, it is to always seek a second opinion. While a vast majority of physicians will not intentionally misdiagnose you for financial gain, doctors can still make mistakes. Often, medical treatment can bring about a series of complications that extend past the severity of the disease itself. As such, it's important to ensure that the diagnosis is a true positive, which is more likely to occur when you consult multiple professionals. You are your greatest advocate, so be sure to maintain a skeptical optimism when receiving medical advice and/or direction.

CHAPTER 5:
DEADLY DISHONESTY

ON THE SHOULDERS OF DWARVES

While a majority of our faith in the healthcare system tends to be directly placed toward the doctors, nurses, and other medical professionals who treat us, the fundamental ethical and treatment standards on which these professionals practice is actually based upon scientific and clinical research. In other words, if your physician can be thought to be the tip of a pyramid, the bricks on which all else rests upon is ongoing medical research. Therefore, it stands to reason that this foundation must be resolute and impregnable. It should be noted at this point, however, that research is dynamic and, as such, ever-changing. Perhaps a more apt analogy would be a complex electrical circuit that must be systematically managed and serviced to ensure all components operate in an effective and efficient manner– replacing parts with new, updated pieces for superior functionality. You wouldn't expect your plumber or electrician to cut proverbial corners or use inferior products to fix your sink or rewire your home. In the same way, the scientific and medical communities uphold a strict set of ethical and quality-control standards to ensure studies are reliable and, subsequently, work toward the benefit of good patient outcomes and overall public health. Unfortunately, the subject of this anecdote disregarded these standards. This decision would go on to spark the beginning of one of the most malignant conspiracy theories of all time; the infamous "anti-vaxx" movement.

On February 28, 1998, Andrew Wakefield, a British gastroenterologist, along with some of his colleagues published a research study in the world-renowned medical journal The Lancet. In this paper, now permanently marked as RETRACTED for clear scientific inaccuracies, poor study design and execution, as well as blatant ethical violations, Wakefield laid out an argument connecting the measles-mumps-rubella (MMR) vaccine to the development of autism spectrum disorder in pediatric patients. More explicitly, Wakefield noticed that eight of his pediatric patients demonstrated signs of intestinal inflammation which he believed to be directly associated with the administration of the MMR vaccine. Because of this apparent intestinal inflammation, the now disgraced doctor associated an increase in intestinal permeability to the hematogenous spread of normally non-permeable neurotoxic peptides, which eventually progressed to the brain and effected development. While the former physician's hypothesis itself is certainly permissible regarding the nature of the scientific method, the interpretation of the study's so-called "data" was highly questionable, if not flagrantly dishonest.

In most, if not all, experimental and observational studies, researchers include control subjects; Wakefield and his colleagues, however, did not. Typically, control subjects are used to determine whether the experimental subjects or groups can be correlated with a respective experimental variable. That is to say, if I were to ask whether mice lose their hair if given cranberry juice, I would need to have a group of mice, which were given cranberry juice (this would be the experimental group), and another group of mice who were given only water (the control group). If a control group were excluded, I could use only mice with alopecia (a disease that results in autoimmune hair loss) in my experiments and resultantly, and falsely, conclude that cranberry juice does relate to hair loss. Considering that at the time, every month, over 50,000 British children (the population Wakefield was studying) received the implicated MMR vaccine at ages between one and two (the age at which symptoms and signs of autism spectrum disorder [ASD] become apparent), coincidences were not only inevitable, they were guaranteed; in England in 1998, one in 2000 children were diagnosed with ASD. In fact, about twenty-five children a month would receive a diagnosis of ASD shortly after receiving the MMR vaccine by pure chance.

In order to avoid the effects of biases, many studies, particularly those involving drugs, employ a process known as "blinding." In other words, investigators will blind themselves regarding their data in order to avoid applying their own biases to the data and, subsequently, make inappropriate and false conclusions. In this particular case, Wakefield et al. failed to blind themselves regarding the endoscopic and neuropsychological tests they conducted on their cohort (the group of children included in the study). As such, any deviation from "normal" could easily be misconstrued as an effect of the MMR vaccine (whether incidentally true or not). Furthermore, several of the children included in Wakefield's study were diagnosed with autism before any gastrointestinal symptoms began; bringing into question the correlative relationship between vaccination and neurodevelopment dysfunction.

Perhaps the most damning of all, however, arose from the admission by The Lancet that Wakefield and his colleagues had neglected to disclose financial interests regarding their study. Later, it would be revealed that Wakefield was funded by lawyers actively engaged in lawsuits against vaccine-producing companies. Therefore, there was a great deal of economic incentive to "prove" the MMR vaccine had a casual connection to the development of disease. While The Lancet exonerated the researchers involved in the fraudulent study from ethical violations and scientific misconduct, the journal officially retracted the paper in 2010 on the grounds that there were several false elements regarding the investigation. Andrew Wakefield is prohibited from practicing medicine in the United Kingdom, and is not licensed in the US, despite living there.

RESIDUAL RIDICULOUSNESS

While the logical conclusion of this story, especially in the light of the mounting evidence against and near total absence of evidence in support of Wakefield et al., should've been the total disappearance of the false notions presented in the study, there is a progressively increasing number of parents refusing to vaccinate their children. Citing the disgraced physician and his colleagues, parents are claiming health concerns regarding many vaccinations recommended by the American Academy of Pediatrics, British Pediatric Association, and International Pediatric Association. Widely disproven and disregarded on the basis of distinct ethical violations and clear experimental design failures, the Wakefield study gave rise to a multinational movement seeking to discredit the effectiveness of vaccines and falsely implicate such commonly accepted treatments in pathogenicity (the development of disease).

The aftershocks of Wakefield et al.'s unethical actions have significantly contributed to the recent rise in childhood diseases in the West once believed to have been effectively eradicated. Measles, a disease caused by the measles virus, is one such illness that has made such a comeback, particularly in light of the respective vaccination's implication within Wakefield's "research." Despite the fact measles can easily lead to miscarriages, severe birth defects, life-threatening measles encephalopathy (brain swelling, coma, and eventual death in many cases), there are many who still side with the widely disproven and discredited information (or, misinformation, rather) shared by a now unlicensed physician and his equally complicit research colleagues. If not careful, we may very well see other nasty diseases make a return from the pre-vaccine era.

It is difficult for many to understand why a rising number of people are accepting a disgraced physician over commonly accepted medical expert opinion and well-established scientific research. However, in the light of basic human instinct, this phenomenon isn't such a mystery. Much like the seemingly peculiar beliefs that the earth is flat, radio waves cause birds to fall from the sky, or a secret Hollywood cult is using the blood of children as a psychoactive, people tend to believe things that make sense within the range of their spectrum of understanding. That is to say, there is a negative correlation between level of education and gullibility. This is the basic concept, which contributes to the effectiveness of illusions and cons– manipulating simple matters of reality to appear magical or better-than-possible situations.

If I were to explain to a three year old that the sky above is blue because it is made of water, you'd be hard-pressed to find a child of that age that wouldn't believe that notion to be pure truth. Our worldview is limited to our ability to understand the underlying mechanisms and concepts that essentially explain the functioning of this universe we inhabit. It takes more than a decade of university-level education in order to understand vaccines and their effect on population-level control of disease spread. Because such a small number of the world's population has obtained such a high level of schooling, it's not surprising that there are so many willing to believe such absurd myths and conspiracies in the realm of "vaccine-induced autism enterocolitis"–a medical condition that now only exists as a term.

So, how do we solve this discrepancy in biomedical knowledge and its tendency to create gullibility? In short, the answer lies within education. Public and private educational institutions alike should make a better effort to ensure children understand the basics of health and medicine; these are, after all, crucial to a better quality of life. In terms of language, clinical and scientific studies tend to be exclusively presented in biological verbiage, thereby existing as unintelligible for the layman. Those in the scientific and medical communities should work harder to make research results and conclusions more accessible to those lacking the years of knowledge and wisdom necessary to fundamentally understand the information provided.

At the end of the day, the greatest conclusion one can formulate based upon the carefully orchestrated tale told by Wakefield et al. is careful skepticism. If your physician gives you a poor diagnosis, always get a second opinion. If you hear something that you're unsure about, do your own research. Take caution, however, not to fall victim to the same confirmation bias Wakefield and his colleagues participated in. That is to say, when researching or getting a second opinion, don't exclusively seek out sources that will give you what you want to hear, search for confirmed, peer-reviewed resources and experienced experts in their field for wise counsel. In the words of one of the wisest people who ever lived, King Solomon, "The way of a fool is right in his own eyes, but a wise man listens to advice," and "Where there is no guidance, a people falls, but in an abundance of counselors there is safety."

REFERENCES

◉ Borowski, John. *The Strange Case of Dr. H.H. Holmes.* (2005).

◉ Chapin, H. Gerald. "A Study in the Fine Art of Murder." *Green Bag 13* (1901): 515.

◉ Corbitt, Robert L. *The Holmes Castle: A Story of H.F. Holmes' Mysterious Work.* Corbitt & Morrison, 1895.

◉ Crighton, J. D., and Herman Webster Mudgett. *Holmes' Own Story: Confessed 27 Murders, Lied Then Died.* Aerobear Classics, 2016.

◉ "Do No Harm." Dateline NBC. 17 Jan. 2015. NBC.

◉ Fleming, Peter, and Stelios C. Zyglidopoulos. "The escalation of deception in organizations." *Journal of Business Ethics* 81.4 (2008): 837-850.

◉ Gilmore, John. *Severed: The True Story of the Black Dahlia*. Amok Books, 2006.

◉ Haugen, Brenda. *The Black Dahlia: Shattered Dreams*. Capstone, 2010.

◉ Hodel, Steve. *Black Dahlia Avenger: The True Story*. Simon and Schuster, 2012.

◉ "Holmes Cool to the End." *The New York Times*. 9 May 1896.

◉ Kerns, Rebecca, Tiffany Lewis, and Caitlin McClure. "Herman Webster Mudgett." *Unpublished raw data, Department of Psychology, Radford University, Radford, VA* (2012).

◉ Larson, Erik. *The devil in the white city: Murder, magic, and madness at the fair that changed America*. Vintage, 2004.

◉ Michas, F. (2019, May 21). Minutes US oncologists spend with each Patient 2018. Retrieved from https://www.statista.com/statistics/606327/oncologist-patient-minutes-spent-gender/

◉ Nisbett, Richard E., and Timothy D. Wilson. "The halo effect: evidence for unconscious alteration of judgments." *Journal of personality and social psychology* 35.4 (1977): 250.

◉ Njambi, S., et al. "Fungal neuroinfections: rare disease but unacceptably high mortality." *Neuro endocrinology letters* 28 (2007): 25.

◉ "Painful Greed Turns Deadly." *American Greed*, narrated by Stacy Keach, Season 13, Episode 10, CNBC, 27 Jan. 2020.

◉ Plotkin, Stanley, Jeffrey S. Gerber, and Paul A. Offit. "Vaccines and autism: a tale of shifting hypotheses." *Clinical Infectious Diseases* 48.4 (2009): 456-461.

◉ Rao, TS Sathyanarayana, and Chittaranjan Andrade. "The MMR vaccine and autism: Sensation, refutation, retraction, and fraud." Indian journal of psychiatry 53.2 (2011): 95.

◉ Schechter, Harold. *Depraved: The Definitive True Story of H.H. Holmes, Whose Grotesque Crimes Shattered Turn-Of-the-Century Chicago*. Simon and Schuster, 2004.

◉ Von Hippel, William, and Robert Trivers. "The evolution and psychology of self-deception." *Behavioral and brain sciences* 34.1 (2011): 1.